The Craft of Writing

Cavendish Square
New York

Journalism

JULIE A. EVANS

Published in 2012 by Cavendish Square Publishing, LLC
303 Park Avenue South, Suite 1247, New York, NY 10010

First Edition

Website: cavendishsq.com

This publication represents the opinions and views of the author based on his or her personal experience, knowledge, and research. The information in this book serves as a general guide only. The author and publisher have used their best efforts in preparing this book and disclaim liability rising directly or indirectly from the use and application of this book.

CPSIA Compliance Information: Batch #WR314260CSQ

All websites were available and accurate when this book was sent to press.

Library of Congress Cataloging-in-Publication Data
Evans, Julie A. • Journalism / Julie A. Evans. • p. cm.—(The craft of writing)
Includes bibliographical references and index. • Summary: "Explores the craft of journalistic writing in the formats of newspaper, magazine, and online"—Provided by publisher.
ISBN 978-1-60870-498-9 (print) • ISBN 978-1-60870-650-1 (ebook) • 1. Journalism—
Authorship. 2. Reporters and reporting. I. Title. • PN4775.E93 2011 • 808'.06607—dc22 •
2010048839

Publisher: Michelle Bisson • Art Director: Anahid Hamparian
Series Designer: Alicia Mikles • Photo research by Lindsay Aveilhe

Printed in the United States of America

Contents

Introduction 5

1. History of Journalism 9

2. The Big Picture 28

3. From First Idea to Finish 49

4. Finding Your Niche 68

5. Putting It All Together 75

Glossary 78

Timeline 81

Notes 85

Further Information 89

Bibliography 90

Index 91

MUTUAL FUND PERFORMANCE
Continued from A9

Total meltdown

Dow plunges a record 777

markets take a reco

Crisis

bailout Monday sent the S&P 500

centage loss since October 1987 and cost investors

$1.2 trillio

arties

scue fails

nt bankers feel the
at once-flush firms

for money market funds, curbs on 'short sales' sought

Stocks

ble amid new Wall St et landscape

Economic woes

Wall Street braces for

FINANCIAL SYSTEM IN CRISIS

Tension
around

00,000,

It's an 'extremely worrisome situa

Angs

can't find
economic
footing

INVESTING

Money
market
fund
falters

d to '

rly half of sales
w foreclosures

the course

dive

FINANCIAL SYSTEM IN CRISIS

Long, dark tunnel seen

pens amid

More pain for buyers

Introduction

IT'S AN EXCITING TIME TO BE A JOURNALIST.

Over the past decade, major changes have taken place in the way news is packaged and presented to readers. This is because of the rise of the Internet. Available 24/7, the Internet brings breaking news and constant updates to readers who are just a click away from the next big story or news video.

As a news medium, the Internet is in crowded and competitive company. Nine out of ten Americans rely on multiple news sources, including local and national television, newspapers, radio, and the Internet, according to the Pew Internet & American Life Project. (The project is part of the Pew Research Center, a nonpartisan, nonprofit organization that provides information on attitudes and trends

People go into journalism for all kinds of reasons—but one reason is key: Journalism makes a difference!

in society.) According to the Pew study, people's relationship to news is becoming more and more portable (via cell phones and laptops), personalized (home pages customized with favorite news sites), and participatory (commenting on news and sharing it on Facebook, for example).

News is also becoming more "democratic"—anyone with Internet access can weigh in on the public conversation via blogs, e-mail, Twitter, Digg, Facebook, or any number of social-media tools.

As technology plays an ever greater role in the delivery and presentation of news, the academic world of journalism education has had to adapt to and embrace the digital age. Although the basic elements of journalism—reporting, interviewing, critical thinking, writing, objectivity, and ethics —are the same as they've always been, people who wish to study journalism today will use technologies that didn't exist ten years ago.

As an aspiring journalist, you will learn to present news as a total package by combining text, audio, video, links, and share features. But that isn't all. You will also be expected to capture and edit audio, video, and still shots using Final Cut Pro and Audacity; to work with chat capabilities; to interact with readers via social media; and to design layouts with Dreamweaver, InDesign, and other software.

Journalism programs are on the rise in colleges and universities. If you want to be in the top tier of the profession, you'll need to learn the technology. But you will still have to excel in the basic skills of reporting and writing.

This book will help you acquire the skills you need and get early experience as a journalist.

Why Study Journalism?

Don't forget the reason most people enter the field in the first place—journalism matters.

A responsible and independent news media is necessary to develop and maintain a healthy democracy. The public relies on reporters to search for information and inform the public about all aspects of society—government, business, economics, academics, science, health, the military, culture, sports, and more. Journalists stay on top of news "beats" and alert the public to corruption within government, business, organized religion, and other powerful institutions. They inform about public policy and laws, and provide information so that the public can decide which ideas have merit and which ones do not.

Information from a free press also helps consumers make decisions that guide their daily lives—what to do during a flu outbreak, for example: where to send children to school; what foods provide the most nutrition; and which political candidate has ideas that reflect or challenge our own.

Consider the alternative: without a free press, government leaders could rule without regard for citizens' best interests. Unless exposed by an aggressive "watchdog" media, business leaders can put personal interests ahead of both shareholders' priorities and public safety. Without reporters asking tough questions, corruption would increase, the cost of doing business would rise, and citizens would lose even more trust in government than they already have.

Most people who go into journalism do so because they love to write. But they also love chasing down leads, interviewing people, learning about new ideas, and racing to make deadline. Few go into journalism for the money. With low to average pay, long hours, and often pretty tough assignments, journalism truly is a labor of love.

History of Journalism

REMEMBER THE CHILDHOOD GAME called "telephone"? A group of children gather in a circle. The first player whispers a sentence to the next player, who then whispers to the next player, and so on, until everyone is in on the news. Or are they? When the last player reveals the whispered sentence to the entire group, it's usually very different from the original sentence.

The earliest days of journalism seem a lot like a game of telephone. Before there were newspapers, the first "reporters" spread news by word of mouth, which may have taken days, weeks, or months to deliver. Accuracy depended on the amount of news to share, as well as the ability of the person reporting the news to recall key facts.

Historians generally credit Julius Caesar with creating the first published news, called *Acta Diurna* (*Daily Events*), around 59 BCE. News of war, legal proceedings, births, deaths, and other public information was carved

Though he became known as a fictional character, Vlad Tsepes Drakul, the ruler of Transylvania in 1456–1462, was first heard of through news reports about his abuse of the Germans in his country.

on stone or metal and displayed for public viewing. In the eighth century, the first known newspapers appeared in Beijing as handwritten news sheets.

The invention of the printing press in 1447 paved the way for the mass production of news reports. By the late fifteenth century, news sheets could be found in Germany; one even reported on the abuse that Germans in Transylvania suffered at the hands of Vlad Tsepes Drakul, better known as Count Dracula.

By the 1620s, a variety of newspapers were circulating in central Europe, and after 1650, newspapers became the most widely read nonreligious material.

Journalism—American Style

America's first newspaper was published in Boston in 1690. More than three centuries later, there are approximately 1,400 daily newspapers in the United States. The largest, *The Wall Street Journal*, boasts a circulation of more than 2 million readers. While newspapers hold the longest tradition of news gathering and reporting, they compete with—and have lost readers to—news magazines, radio, television, and the Internet.

The decades ahead will bring many changes and challenges to the news industry, including what's considered newsworthy and how news is delivered to readers. To understand both journalism today and its probable future, it helps to look back at journalism's earliest days and its evolution from propaganda and sensationalism to more objective and balanced news reporting

In the late 1630s, the first printing press arrived in America, not long after English settlers established colonies in Virginia and Massachusetts. In 1690, the first newspaper to be published in America, *Publick Occurrences, Both Forreign and Domestick*, debuted in Boston, with sensational stories of scandal and murder. The paper was shut down after only one issue, and all copies were destroyed because its publisher failed to get a license to publish from the English monarchy. While its sensational style didn't win favor with royalty in England, it did set the tone for future newspapers, which also gave plenty of ink to stories of war, crime, sex, and disaster, in an ongoing series of bids to win over readers.

In 1721, James Franklin (Benjamin's brother) established the *New England Courant*. The paper challenged religious and political authorities, setting a precedent for future journalists. In fact, Franklin's harsh criticisms of colonial government authorities landed him in jail; brother Benjamin took over. Two years after its first edition, the *New England Courant* was shut down and banned by authorities.

By the beginning of the Revolutionary War, there were about two dozen newspapers in the colonies. Many articles were used as propaganda to sway public opinion toward political independence from England. By 1783, at war's end, there were forty-three newspapers.

Birth of the Free Press

Historians mark the beginning of America's free-press tradition with the 1734 trial of John Peter Zenger, who was charged with seditious libel.

Libel is the act of presenting information that is known to be false, in print or some other medium. It usually involves public figures, such as government officials or celebrities. But in colonial America, laws prohibiting libel meant that you couldn't print anything bad about the government or its leaders, even if it proved to be true.

That's how Zenger got himself into big trouble with the law. As publisher of the *New York Weekly Journal*, Zenger published comments that were critical of William Cosby, the British governor of New York. Zenger was arrested and thrown in jail for these remarks.

At trial, Zenger was defended by Andrew Hamilton, whose brother was Alexander Hamilton, a man who

John Peter Zenger was originally apprenticed to William Bradford of the *New York Gazette.* This early cartoon gets its facts wrong; something of which Zenger himself was found not guilty.

would become one of America's Founding Fathers. Hamilton argued that published statements about the governor weren't libelous *if they were true.* This kind of press freedom was a new idea for the times and challenged existing laws concerning what you could and couldn't say in print.

The jury returned a verdict of "not guilty." Zenger was released from prison and went back to work at his newspaper with the freedom to write about the government and its leader, even if the governor didn't approve of the content.

This began a nationwide movement toward freedom of the press, which continued until the close of the Revolutionary War and the establishment of the Bill of Rights, including the First Amendment, in 1791.

First Amendment: Congress shall make no law respecting an establishment of religion, or prohibiting the free exercise thereof; or abridging the freedom of speech, or of the press; or the right of the people peaceably to assemble, and to petition the Government for a redress of grievances.

Industrial Revolution and Beyond

By the 1800s, the United States had entered a period of swift technological progress that made modern media possible. The Industrial Revolution changed society from one that was primarily agricultural to one based on manufacturing and industry. Inventions such as the steamship, railroad, and telegraph made communicating across the country and overseas faster. The development of the high-speed printing press helped to keep printing costs down.

With the introduction of what was called the "penny press" in the 1830s, newspaper circulations quickly shifted from a small upper-class readership to a mass readership. With papers selling for just one cent per copy, a larger and more diverse group of readers began to demand news. The content of the "Penny Press" newspapers still focused on sensational stories of crime and scandal, but they tailored news coverage to the average citizen instead of the upper classes. To that end, the papers used more colorful words and shorter sentences, and often printed invented news stories to draw readers. As cities and industry grew, publishers began to see the newspaper as an attractive way to make money.

The mid–1800s were a busy time for newspaper entrepreneurs. Daily newspapers such as the *New York Times*, the *Baltimore Sun*, and the *Chicago Tribune* were founded in the 1850s. (Mark Twain, later America's most famous satirist, got his start in journalism in the 1860s as a features writer for a newspaper in Virginia City.) Joseph Pulitzer and William Randolph Hearst, two men who would go on to become media titans, began building newspaper empires in the second half of the nineteenth century, after the end of the Civil War in 1865. Their fierce competition for readers resulted in "yellow journalism"—sensational reporting about crime, sex, disaster, gossip, and questionable scientific discoveries, all aimed at attracting readers.

Like the "penny papers" earlier in the century, the newspapers of Pulitzer (*New York World*) and Hearst (*New York Journal*) were filled with exciting stories in hopes of luring readers. Unlike those earlier newspapers, the *World* and *Journal* refrained from completely making up stories. They did, however, "create" news.

For example, *World* reporter Elizabeth Cochrane (a.k.a. Nellie Bly) circled the globe by boat and train in an attempt to beat the fictional record of Phileas Fogg in Jules Verne's classic novel, *Around the World in Eighty Days*. She made the journey in seventy-two days, and filed news reports during her travels.

Changes Underway

At the turn of the century, calls for press reform led to major changes in how both journalists and journalism were viewed. There were some concerns that powerful people, like Hearst and E. W. Scripps, were controlling the press and news coverage through the newspaper chains they were building.

Upper-class readers criticized newspapers for pandering to working-class values and for sensational coverage, lowering moral standards, and encouraging class hatred rather than educating and cultivating readership. There were calls for "news" to be kept separate from "opinion." And there was an increasing demand for journalists who were well educated and of high moral integrity.

But changes in journalism didn't occur until the industry was faced with the sobering impact of both World War I and the Great Depression. As the stock market crashed, many tabloids went out of business or changed to more serious reporting. However, newspaper reporters still covered stories of celebrity scandals and intrigue, such as the kidnapping of the Lindbergh baby.

Though competition for news about the kidnapping of the Lindbergh baby was so fierce that at least one journalist planted false evidence, the newspapers also reported accurately on the arrest of Bruno Hauptmann, who took the baby.

Journalists from all over the country traveled to Hopewell, New Jersey, in 1932 after the son of famous aviator Charles Lindbergh disappeared from the family's nursery. Competition for breaking news was fierce—several journalists even planted fake evidence near the crime scene and brought a photographer along to document it as police "discovered" the new evidence that wasn't really evidence. Another journalist planted incriminating evidence at the apartment of the man accused of kidnapping and killing baby Lindbergh. The journalist was caught after bragging about his actions to friends.

Viewers Tune In to Broadcast Journalism

By the 1920s, radio had begun to secure its spot as a permanent news medium in American journalism. Unlike newspapers, radio brought people together and created a connection to the larger world. People in rural Tennessee could tune into the same broadcast as people in Los Angeles or New York. Worried about the competition, many newspaper publishers refused to print radio broadcast schedules. The American Newspaper Publishers Association tried to force radio out of the news business. And the Associated Press forbade its members from releasing news to radio stations.

As American listeners proved that radio was here to stay, however, many news companies gave up on sabotage and began investing in the new medium. By 1941, more than 30 percent of American radio stations were at least partly owned by newspapers, and there were nearly one thousand commercial radio stations operating in the United States.

Newspaper publishers were a lot less worried when television arrived in the 1940s. Television was seen as an entertainment vehicle that also happened to provide some news. Many radio broadcasters transitioned into TV with relative ease. But radio reporters were a different story. Accustomed to being the "voice" and not the "face" behind the news, some journalists objected to the new, on-camera format.

The year 1949 was pivotal for broadcast journalism, including the introduction of 16 mm film and the Tele-

PrompTer, a device that scrolled the newscast, allowing reporters to read the news while looking at the camera.

Broadcast journalism went on to revolutionize the world. From the Nixon-Kennedy presidential debates, which many think changed the public's opinion of whom to vote for during the 1960 election, to the televised scenes of the war in Vietnam, which brought down a president, to the Watergate hearing, which brought down another, being able to "see" the news has changed the world.

After Richard M. Nixon appeared on national television during a presidential debate looking pale and blowing his nose, elections were never the same. Voters now cared not just about what candidates said and how they said it, but how good they looked while expressing their opinions on the issues of the day.

Citizen Journalism

On the morning of April 16, 2007, no member of the media knew that a major news event was going to unfold that day. So when armed Virginia Tech University student Seung-Hui Cho entered Norris Hall and opened fire on unsuspecting students and faculty, there was no professional camera crew to document the event.

However, graduate student Jamal Albarghouti did document it. As police officers ran past him and into Norris Hall, Albarghouti hit the ground and then used his cell phone to record video and audio footage of the officers reacting to Cho's gunshots. When he made it back to his computer, Albarghouti uploaded the video to CNN's iReport website, which was created in 2006 with the purpose of allowing any person, anywhere, to upload videos, write news stories, and discuss news events happening around them. This site gave Albarghouti the opportunity to upload his video, which in turn provided the media with footage of a major news event as it was still unfolding.

Albarghouti's cell phone video was frequently aired to illustrate television news reports about the Virginia Tech massacre, and is today considered the most memorable video of the horrific event. Although this was a tragic day, it is also the day that proved citizen journalism has the ability to enhance and inform media coverage.

The cell phone used by graduate student Jamal Albarghouti to record the massacre at Virginia Tech in 2007 is now on display at the Newseum in Washington, D.C. The Newseum is dedicated to the history of the news.

Technology Prompts Rapid Changes . . . Again

In the past decade or so, journalism has undergone another major transformation, thanks to the Internet. The technology of journalism is changing so rapidly that it is difficult to predict all the ways that news will be delivered in just a few years.

Digital technology—joined by innovation and entrepreneurial energy—is presenting new possibilities for reporters. Good reporting still requires journalists to dig deep for information and to get out and talk to sources. But the Internet gives journalists the ability to update their work throughout the day, verify facts more easily, and communicate more directly with readers.

> " Technology is changing the economics of journalism. In radio and television time is limited. In print journalism space is limited. But on the Internet there is essentially an unlimited amount of time and an unlimited amount of space. The limitation is the attention span of the Internet users. "
> —Vinton G. Cerf, Vice President and Chief Internet Evangelist, Google

In fact, one of the biggest shifts in the last decade has been the increasing involvement of the reader through e-mail, blogs, Twitter, Facebook, Digg, and mobile uploads, to name a few.

The rise of *citizen journalism* also has been moving the reader into the territory of the professional journalist. Citizen journalism happens when the average citizen—usually without formal journalism training—reports, writes, fact-checks, produces, and posts news stories using the tools of modern technology, especially the Internet.

Many news executives now embrace the Internet. In fact, the survival of many print publications may depend on how quickly and completely they adapt to ever-changing technology and become leaders in Internet publishing.

America's Brave Journalists

Elijah Lovejoy (1802–1837): Lovejoy used his press in Illinois to work toward the abolition of slavery. Angry mobs who opposed his views destroyed three of his presses, but Lovejoy continued to defend his right to publish. He was killed as he tried to stop a mob from setting fire to the warehouse where he stored his newly delivered fourth press.

"Nellie Bly" (1867–1922): A pseudonym for Elizabeth Cochrane, a reporter who told stories of ordinary people, often by going undercover. She once faked insanity to get into an insane asylum and report on conditions there. On another assignment, she traveled around the world in seventy-two days to beat a record of eighty days.

Elizabeth "Nellie Bly" Cochrane was one of the first investigative reporters in the United States. She often went "undercover" to get her stories, a practice that is both admired and vilified by modern-day journalists.

Martha Gellhorn (1908–1998): Gellhorn was a war correspondent during some of the most important conflicts of the twentieth century, including the Spanish Civil War, World War II, and the Vietnam War. Married to Ernest Hemingway, Gellhorn snuck aboard a hospital ship to witness the D-Day landings in Normandy during World War II.

Ernie Pyle (1900–1945): This popular war correspondent covered America's involvement in World War II from the front lines in North Africa, Sicily, Italy, and France. Pyle's columns appeared in approximately four hundred daily and three hundred weekly newspapers. His columns gave readers an inside look at war. He admired the courage of soldiers doing battle. In 1945, Pyle was killed by sniper fire on the Japanese island of Ie Shima.

Margaret Bourke-White (1904–1971): One of the world's most famous photojournalists, Bourke-White used photography and the photo essay to document the Great Depression. During World War II, she was the only woman permitted in war zones by the U.S. Army. Bourke-White interviewed and photographed Mohandas K. Gandhi a few hours before his assassination in India. She is credited with starting the first photo lab at LIFE magazine.

Carl Bernstein and **Bob Woodward** (1944– ; 1943–): *Washington Post* reporters Bernstein and Woodward worked as a team to investigate the June 1972 break-in at the Democratic National Committee's office in the Watergate complex, in Washington, D.C. Through persistent reporting, they uncovered President Richard M. Nixon's involvement in the break-in. Their work won a Pulitzer Prize for the *Washington Post* for outstanding public service. They later published two books on Watergate: *All the President's Men* (which was made into a movie) and *The Final Days*.

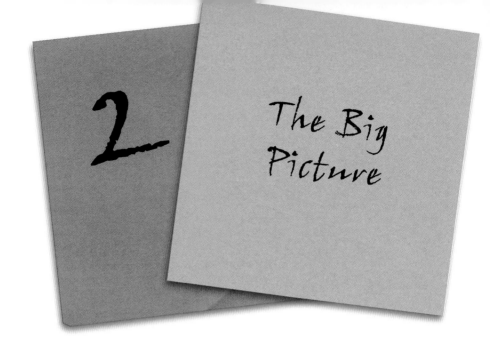

2 — The Big Picture

SUCCESSFUL JOURNALISTS LOVE THE NEWS. They read newspapers, magazines, and online news stories. Journalists listen to news on the radio and watch it on TV. They are curious about the world around them and question everything: How do things work? Why did something happen? Who is responsible? Where did events take place? What is going to happen? What *did* happen?

Many great journalists grew up as the "nosy" kids on the block—the ones who were always being scolded for asking too many questions or eavesdropping on the conversation of others. Like nosy kids and nosy neighbors, journalists want answers to questions that most people don't bother to ask.

It's the ingredients that go into a news story—finding fresh ideas, researching a topic, and interviewing sources—that make journalism such a challenging and rewarding career.

Persistence is another important characteristic of journalists. Good journalists don't stop digging for facts and sources until they're certain that they have all the information they need to write the most factually accurate and complete news story possible.

Where It All Begins

Whether you're interested in covering news for the Internet, your local newspaper, a blog, magazine, or a television or radio network, basic journalism begins with reporting and writing news.

While covering a story, reporters investigate leads (kernels of information that could turn into a larger story), read through relevant documents, research published stories on the topic, interview key people, and observe events at the site, such as a fire or crime scene, or as they unfold, such as a political campaign. All the while, reporters are taking notes—writing down observations and quotes from the people they interview. They also may take photographs or shoot videos. Once they've accumulated enough information, they organize the material, determine and shape the article's focus, and, finally, write the story.

For breaking news, reporters may write stories on laptops at the scene and submit them to the editor electronically. More and more often, news reporters are asked to contribute to a newspaper's website, or write for a newspaper that only exists as a website.

Reporters at large newspapers usually specialize in a particular type of news (called a news beat), such as sports, education, health, city government, politics, crime, and the courts. Reporters on small publications cover all aspects of the news. They also take photographs, write headlines, and even prepare news pages, including story placement, for publication.

If you're looking for a story to cover, often you need look no farther than your local community. This reporter is interviewing a police officer about another police officer who was slain in the line of duty.

Where to Find Story Ideas

- **Immerse yourself in news.** You'll develop a much better "nose for news" if you read newspapers every day. Go to the local library, or access a news website, and read the newspapers from first page to last. Pay attention to story placement—why do some stories merit front-page coverage while other stories get buried deep inside the paper?

- **Look for the little details** that could lead to a bigger story. Reporters often find worthy ideas within other news stories. For example, a front-page news story about a tornado that touches down nearby could be expanded to include news about area businesses that were hurt by the storm or pet owners whose pets were lost in the storm. Or you may come up with a heartwarming story about people coming together to help tornado victims.

- For quirky news stories, **think outside the box**. Scan your town's Craigslist website for headlines that catch your eye, read the article, and follow up to see if there is any weight to the story. Perhaps that woman who lost her engagement ring and created a help wanted ad has a great backstory—what if the ring is a family heirloom? Or her fiancé is fighting in Afghanistan and he proposed right before he left? This is a great way to hone your nose for news and gives you practice in finding leads, following up with sources, and developing

what could be a great story that would other-
wise go unnoticed.

- **Stay on top of current events**. Reporters look
  for trends by keeping up with current events
  and finding new angles to freshly report what
  may appear to be a tired story.

- If you have a **talent or expertise** in some area,
  use it for story ideas! If you're on the football team, write about the booster club's lat-
  est fundraiser. If you play chess, profile other
  players competing in the regional chess tour-
  nament. If you love to swim, write about the
  exercise value of swimming or about the long-
  term effects of chlorine on hair.

- **Listen up!** Reporters get ideas through tips,
  observations, conversations with a variety of
  people from all walks of life (coffee shops are
  great for casual chats), and by calling sources
  (people who can supply information about a
  particular topic) and asking for ideas.

- Try your hand at **videojournalism**. Ask a
  friend to videotape an interview between you
  and someone that you consider newsworthy,
  such as the head of the school board, your
  class president, or the manager of the new
  clothing store that's opening in your town.

"I decided on journalism when I was in high school because I love to write, and I'm curious about everything—especially people and why they do what they do.

"I went to journalism school at Kent State University in Ohio and took my first job at a small suburban daily newspaper outside of Cleveland, writing police news and feature stories, covering village councils and local elections, those sorts of things.

"Now I'm a health reporter for Cleveland's daily newspaper, the *Plain Dealer*. After thirty years in the business, work still makes me happy. I get to dig into complicated concepts and unravel them to make life easier for other people. I get to point out flaws in the system and ask that they be fixed. And I get to hang out with all kinds of people: presidential candidates and guys who've lost both their arms and had them reattached and brain surgeons who impersonate Elvis in their spare time. What it comes down to is this: I get paid to listen to some of the greatest stories out there and then tell them again."

—*Diane Suchetka, newspaper reporter*

Who Am I Writing For?

Always think about your audience as you search for newsworthy stories. For example, a student newspaper would provide a different mix of stories than the community paper, even though some stories may overlap. The student newspaper would provide stories of interest to other students and their families, as well as teachers and administrators.

On the other hand, the mix of stories for a community newspaper is much more diverse so it can appeal to everyone—from young readers to senior citizens.

How Do I Research My Story?

With the seeming wealth of free information on the Internet, as well as print sources and the library, it can be hard to know where to start. The subject of your story should provide some strong clues, however. For example, if you're writing a story on the many paths taken by graduating seniors, you'll probably want to start with the Board of Education to gather data such as graduation rates and college enrollment. You'll also want to interview graduating seniors to ask about plans for education, travel, volunteerism, and employment.

Some stories require more digging for facts than others. If you're writing a story on the economic impact of high school football in your community, you probably want to start with the school board and find out how much money is made in ticket and concession stand sales. Contact the neighborhood sporting goods store to ask about the sales of sweatshirts, T-shirts, caps, and other team apparel. Visit or call area restaurants to find out whether business rises or falls on game nights. Brainstorm other ways that football might raise money for the school and the community, and follow up on these ideas.

On the other hand, you may learn that expenses of high school football actually outweigh revenues because of the costs involved in extracurricular activities—expenses such as uniforms, coaching salaries, security, stadium lighting, turf maintenance, and other operating expenses. That doesn't mean you have no story. It just means that you have a different angle to pursue.

In many ways, researching a story is like researching a term paper. You need trustworthy sources and facts that have been checked by experts for accuracy. Possible resources include almanacs, encyclopedias, dictionaries, academic and trade journals, textbooks, government reports, legal documents, and other reference materials. But news stories may require information that's more recent, and more local, than many reference books provide.

Remember, though there is lots of up-to-date information on the Internet, much of it is not accurate. It may not have been fact-checked or it may be an advertisement or press release disguised as a news story, with the intent to get you to buy a product or service. Or it may be well-intentioned, but inaccurate, because the Internet often recycles old and unreliable information.

For the most reliable background information, stick with websites from associations, colleges and universities, hospitals, government sources, and any other groups that offer information from experts you can trust. Don't use information from websites that are selling a product they recommend.

Another valuable way to research is to interview people who know the facts and can comment on them with authority. For example, you could interview a doctor for a story on heart disease, or a police officer for a story on crime in your neighborhood.

Don't worry about over-researching your story. Professional reporters try to learn as much as they can about a topic. It's better to know more about your subject than you can use than to leave big gaps of information in your story. The best journalists always want to make one more call and check with one more source before deadline.

How Do I Interview People?

Perhaps one of the most challenging skills for a beginning reporter to learn is how to interview a source for a story. Here are some techniques that reporters use to get the information and quotes they need for a good story.

Make an appointment. Call or send an e-mail to the person you'd like to interview, letting them know why you're interested in speaking with them (for example, "I'm writing a story about the history of football at our school, and I understand that you were a player on one of the top teams"). Then set a time and place for the interview, either by phone or in person. If you're looking for a quick quote to support a news story, then a phone interview is probably all you need.

But if you're writing a feature article that requires in-depth questions and answers, then you will want to interview that person face-to-face.

Research your subject. There's nothing more embarrassing than asking questions about something you know nothing about. It's okay that you're not an expert on the subject, you should at least develop a basic understanding of your topic before you start asking questions.

By preparing in advance, you'll be able to skip questions that can be answered by an assistant, or found in a published document. Before the interview, ask your source—the person who has given you background information or tipped you off about the story—to suggest some background reading materials that might help you prepare for the interview. The person being interviewed will appreciate your interest.

Write down your questions in advance. This lets the person you're interviewing know that you are truly taking the assignment seriously. Avoid questions that can be answered with a simple "yes" or "no."

Relax. Maintain eye contact and listen carefully to the answers. Smile when appropriate. That will help you to put the person at ease. When the person you're interviewing is speaking, be sure to nod or make a brief comment to show that you're listening. Lean forward to project an eager and interested attitude.

Take good notes. If you're conducting the interview by phone, write down your notes in a notebook or type them into a text document as the person answers. You want to be sure that you quote the person accurately in the story. If you don't understand something, just ask!

For longer interviews, you may want to use an audio recorder, but be sure to take notes, too, since audio recorders have been known to malfunction during interviews. Always check the batteries before the interview, as batteries can die midsentence, which you're not likely to discover until the end of the interview. If you're using a tape recorder, bring an extra tape, and always bring pens and a notebook to write down notes just in case the recorder malfunctions.

Don't try to write down every word your source says. That will slow things down and make it difficult for you to focus on the conversation. But do jot down the highlights with as much abbreviation as possible.

It is important to listen closely to the person you are interviewing; it's essential to take good notes.

Even though you have already researched and thought up questions to ask during the interview, you do not have to stick to the questions. Focus on what the source is saying, not on what you will ask next. Your next question will be so much better if you've heard the answer to the last one. Sometimes questions that are spontaneous instead of prepared makes for a much better interview, with vivid detail and rich quotes. But don't abandon your prepared questions—use them to guide the interview if the conversation begins to lag.

When the interview is over, take a few minutes to write down everything you remember about the person (how he or she is dressed, which mannerisms stand out) and the setting of the interview so that you can add colorful details to the story. For example, "I met Will Hopkins in the library. When I arrived, he was sitting at a table, reading glasses covering his large blue eyes, looking through one of many books."

What's Quoteworthy, Anyway?

As previously noted, quotes add interest and color, and let the reader know that you've interviewed someone who's closely involved with the story. But what makes something quoteworthy?

People don't always speak clearly or in a well-organized manner that's directly to the point. Almost always, you'll have to listen to more words than you can print.

The trick is to learn to recognize quotable statements. The quote should move the story forward, not repeat information that you've already written. For example, you're writing a story about a cat that ran up a giant oak tree. You wouldn't quote the cat's owner as saying, "Tiger ran up the tree." Instead, you might write the following: The calico cat ran up the tree and refused to come down. The owner wasn't worried until a buzzard perched on the tree branch above the cat. "The buzzard was staring at Tiger, and I just knew he was going to try and eat her." That was when she made the decision to call the fire department. "I know that's so cliché, but I didn't know what else to do!"

If something doesn't read well and isn't "quote-worthy," but you'd like to include the information, you can paraphrase it (remove the quotes but attribute the information to the person who's speaking.) Let's imagine that you've interviewed the class president about this year's biggest fund-raiser. The president tells you, "This fund-raiser should be great. I just hope that we can raise enough money to continue to fund important stuff." This quote doesn't explain the meaning of "stuff." But later in the interview, the president tells you that the fund-raiser provides scholarship money to a student who excels at academics and sports. You would paraphrase by writing, "Class president Mark Derrickson says money raised by the "Dunk the Principal" fund-raiser will be used to pay for a scholarship to a deserving student who excels at academics and sports."

Check Your Facts

Accuracy is key to good journalism. Many errors can be prevented by checking simple facts:

Check the spelling of proper names and make sure names are spelled consistently throughout the story. Never assume that you know how to spell a name. For example: Shawn and Sean are pronounced the same way yet have different spellings. Same goes for Cathy, Kathie, and Kathy.

Read back to the interviewee the spelling of his or her name, even if the name is as simple and easy as Bob (and find out whether "Bob" would prefer to be called "Robert"). Ask sources if they use a middle name or middle initial.

Give full company names (again, don't guess or assume spelling.) If you're including a URL, be sure to type it into your Web browser to make sure it's accurate.

Make sure to take the time to check all your facts before handing in a story; it'll make all the difference to your reputation as a serious journalist.

Confirm dates with your sources.

Check all numbers. Think like a math student. Be on the lookout for misplaced decimal points and commas. If you're using percentages in a story (e.g., "50 percent of Americans prefer coffee, 30 percent prefer tea, and 20 percent prefer soda"), make sure they add up to 100 percent.

If you need to include someone's age, ask for a birth date and year.

Be sure to get your source's phone number and e-mail address so that you can contact this person again, if you need to ask more questions or verify information from the interview.

Fair and Balanced Reporting

A note on balance and objectivity: your job as a journalist is to report facts and the opinions of others. Unless you're writing an editorial, critical review, letter to the editor, or blog entry, you need to leave your opinions out of the story.

And make sure to add balance. If you are writing a story about school lunches and nutrition, and you quote someone who claims that school lunches are bad for you, then ask to see a menu and nutritional information for a month's worth of lunches. Interview a nutritionist who can discuss the menu and its nutritional value. Let the reader decide based on the facts that you present. Balance is a must. Readers will feel cheated if you slant the facts or fail to present a fair representation of opposing viewpoints.

Although this sounds simple, balance is sometimes hard to find, especially in stories about situations typically frowned upon by society. For example, if you're writing a story about violence against women, you probably aren't going to find someone to justify hurting a woman. Instead, only present facts and quotes that can be verified by reputable sources. Keep your voice out of the story.

"I remember meeting up with my fellow students in my freshman year in J school. I wanted to know why they were there. After all, we were all training to do the coolest and most exciting job in the world! I thought we'd make a connection in this common passion for journalism. Then many would inevitably say, 'Math . . . I was never good at math.'

"But that wasn't me. First, journalism isn't a default career choice! You've got to want it bad. Second, I was really good at math. I got it. It got me. And it's a skill that has guided me my entire career. By analyzing statistics and crunching data, I was able to break stories on new trends. I went from general assignment reporting to becoming specialized in consumer and business. When the financial markets melted in late 2008, I was able to explain the economy and the impact to my audience in the months that followed. These days, numbers are my life."

—*Angie Lau,*
Business/Consumer Network Anchor

Putting It All Together

Once you've decided on a story idea, researched the topic, interviewed sources, and checked your facts, you're ready to write your news story. But where do you begin and how do you arrange your facts?

One of the most widely used techniques in news reporting is the "inverted pyramid," in which the most essential facts appear at the top of the story, in the opening or lead paragraph.

The lead section, starting with the lead paragraph, is where you'll find answers to the so-called Five Ws and H of journalism: Who, What, When, Where, Why, and How.

The lead section of the story is followed by paragraphs containing *nonessential* (but still informative and interesting) details that support the story, in descending order of importance. In these paragraphs, you'll find quotes from sources, any relevant statistics, and additional details that support the story and add interest.

It's important to answer as many of the reader's questions as possible in the opening paragraph for a couple of reasons. First, news readers are busy. They skim for information; if they don't find what they need right away, they may move on to the next story. Also, editors are sometimes forced to cut stories down to a couple of paragraphs due to space limitations, and they often cut from the end of the story. If you don't have the essential facts pulled together at the beginning of your story, and the story gets cut, then it no longer makes sense to the reader.

While you have to prepare for the idea that your story might get cut, you need to assume that it won't. Support your lead paragraph with one or two short quotes to add interest to your story. Quotes show the reader that you're not just reciting facts; you've actually spoken with someone who's involved with the story.

Let's say that the editor of your local newspaper has asked you to write a news story about the upcoming school musical, *Dodos, Gorillas and Bears . . . Oh My!* You'll need to gather facts to answer these basic questions:

45

Who is putting on the play? Who are the main actors? Who is directing the play?

What is the name of the musical and what can theatergoers expect?

Where will the play be performed?

When will performances be held (dates and show times)?

Why did the school choose this particular play?

Why is it important for students to attend?

How did the play come together?

This illustrates how the five Ws are used in a story opener (the H comes later):

To celebrate Earth Day [WHY], Roxboro High School students [WHO], will sing and dance some toe-tapping tunes when they bring their performance of *Dodos, Gorillas and Bears . . . Oh My!* [WHAT], to the Roxboro High School stage, [WHERE], on Friday, April 20, at 8 p.m. [WHEN], The performance is free, with the donation of a nonperishable food item.

According to drama teacher Doris Wiley, the students chose *Dodos, Gorillas and Bears . . . Oh My!* to coincide with Earth Day because the play teaches valuable lessons about conservation [WHY].

"We want our students and the community to learn more about our natural resources

Freelance Writing

A growing number of journalists today are freelance writers, which means they're self-employed, and sell their written work to publishers. But first, they must pitch their well-researched ideas to editors in the hope that they will be interested in that particular story.

The best way to break into a freelance writing career is to write for small, local newspapers, magazines, websites, trade publications, or any other established publication available. Publications with larger circulations will take your ideas more seriously if you can show published clips (samples) of your writing.

and, hopefully, become better stewards of the planet," says Wiley.

The play was a schoolwide effort. It was coauthored by students in the Creative Writing Club, which meets on Wednesdays after school. Music teacher Jerry Brodskey composed the original music, which the Challenge Choir will perform [HOW].

As you can see, the first paragraph provides essential facts about the story. The following paragraphs explain and expand on the opening paragraph, with an expert quote that adds interest to the story.

The lead paragraph is where you'll find answers to the so-called Five Ws of journalism: Who, What, When, Where, and Why.

3 From First Idea to Finish

NEWSPAPERS, MAGAZINES, RADIO, television, and more recently, the Internet, provide many career opportunities for journalists. Although each medium requires a different style of writing, they all share one thing: the need for writers who can tell a story with accuracy, organization, clarity, and concise writing. As an aspiring journalist, you will learn to cut through the "fat" of information to get to the meat of any story. You will learn to think critically by considering more than one point of view, and to question every "fact" before handing in a story.

Let's look at some of the elements that go into a news story for three types of media (newspaper, magazine, and Internet). You can see how one topic gets covered in different ways, depending on the type of article and the publication in which it appears.

Journalism

Newspaper Reporting

How would you respond if your teacher told you that you had to write a well-written, organized, factually sound report every day and present it to the class? And that, on occasion, you had to include relevant photos or video that you shot and produced. And, on top of all that, your research, including documents, meetings, and interviews with people you've never met, must be infallible. If you found yourself intrigued by the challenge, and think that researching, reporting, and writing stories every day—as well as learning something new in the process—sounds exciting, then you may be interested in a career as a newspaper reporter.

Newspaper reporters spend a large part of each day investigating news before writing and "filing"—turning in—a story. Large-circulation newspapers usually assign reporters to a news beat. Reporters at newspapers with smaller circulations, including weeklies, typically cover several beats at a time.

Magazines

A magazine exists for almost every hobby and interest. Go to any newsstand and you'll find large-circulation general-interest magazines such as *Entertainment Weekly, Oprah, Rolling Stone, Men's Health*, and *Time* magazines stuffed alongside narrow-interest publications such as *Official Xbox Magazine, Archaeology, Family Tree Magazine*, and *Psychology Today*.

Newspaper reporters are often assigned stories by news editors, who meet at the beginning of the day to decide what to cover, and later in the day to assign each story's placement in the newspaper.

Magazines are often produced weekly or monthly, giving news editors and reporters more time to develop their stories.

Magazine journalism differs from newspaper journalism in several ways. For starters, there's the target audience. While magazines typically appeal to a national audience with a specialized interest in a particular topic, called a niche, such as politics, health, entertainment, or pets, newspapers must appeal to a wider range of ages and interests with a little bit of everything within their local or regional circulation area.

Magazine journalism also allows reporters and writers to take more time to develop stories. With weekly, monthly, or bimonthly deadlines, magazine journalists often can provide readers with more in-depth coverage of issues and trends than newspaper reporters. Magazine journalists also benefit from more time for reflection and analysis before writing a story.

Depending on the magazine, article length may range from approximately fifty words for a small news brief to more than three thousand words for a major feature.

> **"Clear, well-organized writing is absolutely essential for journalism. The more you practice, the better your writing is going to be.**
>
> **"Some of the best journalism students are the ones who have created their own blogs in high school and have practiced writing on a daily or weekly basis. It doesn't have to be hard-core journalism—it can be about music, pop culture, hobbies. The point is that you're getting practice with writing. You're specializing in something. You're thinking about your audience and learning what people will respond to."**
>
> *—Carrie Brown, Ph.D.,*
> *assistant professor of journalism at*
> *the University of Memphis*

Internet

Short and simple. That's what writing for the Internet demands. Unlike newspapers and magazines, which read-

Increasingly, people are getting their news either from online versions of print newspapers or from those that only publish via the Internet.

ers read more slowly, websites tend to attract readers who are in a hurry. The reader knows that more information, somewhere else, is just a click away. So you need to grab their attention with a catchy headline, followed by reporting, called "copy," which neatly summarizes the news. Copy written for the Internet should be short and snappy. As a rule, Internet readers should be able to read one of your sentences without stopping for a breath.

Too often, the fast pace of news-gathering for the Internet results in sloppy and mistake-riddled writing. The traditional rules of writing still apply online, so stay focused on quality writing with accurate information. It will set your news story apart from the rest.

Internet news writers stay on the lookout for related information that can be shared using interactive tools such as clickable links, video, audio, and graphics. For example, a story on a high school football game might include video coverage, as well as links to other stories about the players, coaches, and games.

Getting Started

To create a successful news story for any type of media, reporters start with a lead (opening sentences that pull in the reader), followed by a well-organized story (copy) that supports the lead and holds the audience's attention.

To keep the story exciting, write in an active voice and use strong verbs whenever possible. Sentences written in the passive voice make the reader work harder; however, sentences written in active voice are easier to read and understand. For example, read these two sentences. See how the active voice flows better and uses fewer words to make the same point?

Emily kicked the soccer ball (active).
The soccer ball was kicked by Emily (passive).

Other writing tips: Avoid run-on sentences, clichés, and mixed metaphors. The latter happens when two or more unrelated metaphors or clichés compete in the same sentence or paragraph. For example, "The handwriting is on the wall. He needs to nip this thing in the bud before it spins out of control."

Journalism

"I wish I'd been born with a burning desire to become a journalist. But no. Despite the fact that writing was always what I did best, and that my dad was a city editor and columnist for a major newspaper, and that I grew up in its city room, I resisted writing as a career path. I was forty before I discovered that I wasn't doing what I was born to do.

"Dropping out of college after one semester, I moved to New York City to become an actress. Instead, I ended up working in Macy's Special Events department and from there, joined a public relations firm. Ten years later, I was running a division of a PR agency and making a six-figure salary.

"But I was miserable. The only thing I liked about my job was writing. I took a terrifying leap, quit, and became a write-at-home mom. One day, I met a health book publisher. He needed someone to write chapters for a woman's health book, and I took the assignment.

"That was my 'aha' moment. I loved the topic, the research, and the writing. Turned out, I was a natural. I applied for a writer's job at a health publishing company, despite not having the required college degree. I got the job and thrived. Soon, I was promoted to an editor's spot at the company's health

magazine. Talk about learning on the job! I
didn't even know what editing really meant till
I'd been hired.

"Now, I'm a successful freelance health
journalist. I write magazine articles and
books, mostly about natural healing. I'm a late
bloomer—but a happy one."

— *Sara Altshul,*
freelance health writer and editor

Crafting Your Lead

Think of the lead (commonly spelled "lede" in newsroom
vernacular) as your opening statement. In a few short sentences, this paragraph tells readers why it's worth their
time to read on. A good lede not only entices the reader,
but also helps you write the remainder of your story by
setting the tone, and establishing the story angle.

The lede should include answers to the most essential
facts, or the five Ws and H (discussed in Chapter 2): Who,
What, Where, When, Why, and How. To get started with
your own lede, try describing your news story to a friend
or teacher in as few words as possible. You don't want to
"bury" your lede under too much nonessential information. Tell the reader right away what the story is about and
why it matters.

Here's an example of an effective news lede that grabs
the reader's attention with very few words:

"A healthy seventeen-year-old heart pumped the gift of life through thirty-four-year-old Bruce Murray Friday, following a four-hour transplant operation that doctors said went without a hitch."

—from "It Fluttered and Became Bruce Murray's Heart," Jonathan Bor, *Post-Standard*, May 12, 1984

This actual news lede works because it draws the reader in with its intriguing premise ("a healthy seventeen-year-old heart pumped the gift of life") while quickly providing the most important details: Doctors successfully saved the man's life using a donor heart.

" I have to have a lead or I can't write anything. I have to have my first sentence, because that's my whole piece. That's the tone that says what is this piece about, it's the theme, the thing by which everything hangs. If I don't have that first sentence, I just can't keep going forward. "

— Susan Trausch, Boston Globe "Best Newspaper Writing 1995," Editorial Writing

Supporting Paragraphs

The lead paragraph should be followed by several paragraphs that include details that support the story, in descending order of importance. Each paragraph should relate to the one that comes before and after it. For example, the second paragraph should include the details introduced in your lead paragraph, and if one of Ws was not included in the lead, make sure it is in the second paragraph. To structure your story, ask yourself: What's this story about? What order of events do I need to describe? Do my transitions seem forced, or do they flow naturally?

Make sure that the information you choose to include in your story is relevant to the topic at hand. Don't include irrelevant information just because it's in your notes or you think it's interesting. In other words, if it doesn't help the story, get rid of it. For example, don't tell readers that Murray's mother plays the violin or that his father owns a yacht. Unless the family is famous or the details support the story, the reader doesn't need to know.

Only use credible sources and back up the information you provide with evidence in the form of statistics or quotes. A credible source is someone or something whose words, ideas, or notions are considered to be factual and relevant to the story. Depending on the story, a credible source might include a police officer, doctor, social worker, or immediate family.

Use the active voice with action words to hold your reader's attention.

Here's how the author of the heart transplant story followed up his strong lead (above):

Early Thursday morning, three surgeons at The Presbyterian Hospital lifted Murray's flabby, enlarged heart from his chest cavity and replaced it with a normal heart that had been flown from St. Louis inside an ice-filled beer cooler. . . .

Quotations

Using quotations in a story not only gives it credibility, but also allows someone else to tell the story even though you are writing it. Quotations also provide two sides to the story, prompting the reader to keep reading and to possibly take sides in the debate. What is said in the quotations often reveals something about the person being quoted. They may express an emotion or describe events from a first-person perspective. They also help to break up copy and add interest to the story. Avoid "so-what" quotes and quotes that only state facts. If you can state it better yourself, in your own words, then do so.

"I decided to study journalism for three reasons: I love to write, I love to learn, and I love people. I believe that if you have those passions, then you have all the makings of a great journalist.

"I first became a journalist when I joined my high school's newspaper. Later, I joined my college newspaper as a reporter, and eventually I became its managing editor. I knew there was no other profession for me. I got my degree in journalism fnd went on to work at a newspaper, a magazine, and a website. For the last ten years, I've been a freelance writer.

"Three years ago, I discovered Bollywood movies, which are Hindi-language films from India, and I became a huge fan. So I started a blog called *The Bollywood Ticket: The American Guide to Indian Movies* at *www.thebollywoodticket.com.* Google News and IMDB have chosen my site as a content provider.

"I'm grateful that I've learned technological skills because they've enabled me to self-publish and create my own global media outlet. The old media establishment may be struggling to reinvent itself in the Internet Age, but it's an exciting time, full of new opportunities, for niche media publishers like me."

—*Jennifer Hopfinger,*
blogger and freelance journalist

Real World News Examples

Here's how three types of media—newspapers, magazines, and the Internet—handled news coverage of the BP oil spill, beginning in April 2010:

New York Times (newspaper):
**April 20, 2010—Oil spill in Gulf of Mexico
NEW ORLEANS—An explosion on an oil drilling rig off the coast of southeast Louisiana left at least 3 people critically injured and 11 others missing as of Wednesday night.**

Rescue teams were searching the area in the Gulf of Mexico by helicopter, plane and boat, Coast Guard officials said.

"We have no idea where the 11 unaccounted-for personnel are at this time," Rear Adm. Mary Landry, the commander of the Coast Guard's Eighth District, said at a news conference. . . .

This news lead works because it neatly sums up the tragedy in just one sentence. The following paragraphs further explain the accident and make strong use of quotations to support the story.

Newsweek (magazine):
It was in mid–May that independent scientists— not any of the officials or researchers working for any of the government agencies on scene at the Deepwater Horizon disaster, let alone

BP—first detected the vast underwater plumes of crude oil spreading like Medusa's locks from the out-of-control gusher in the Gulf of Mexico. BP immediately dismissed the reports, and in late May [former] CEO Tony Hayward flatly declared "there aren't any plumes," stopping just short of accusing the scientists of misconduct. Federal officials called the scientists' claim "misleading, premature and, in some cases, inaccurate."

Now it is increasingly clear that the initial reports of undersea oil were right, that life-giving oxygen in the water column is indeed being depleted, and that unless the laws of chemistry have been repealed, dispersants are likely worsening the tentacles of undersea crude. What might have been just another oil spill—albeit a bad one—has been transformed into something unprecedented. . . .

This magazine news story draws in the reader with intrigue and controversy, using words such as "misconduct," and "unprecedented." It also uses highly effective imagery of the disaster — "the vast underwater plumes of crude oil spreading like Medusa's locks" *and* "tentacles of undersea crude."

Yahoo! News (Internet):

NEW YORK—BP holds enough oil in its reserves to single-handedly supply the United

States for two years. It has little debt for a company of its size and makes more money than Apple and Google combined.

So when the White House arm-twisted its executives into setting aside $20 billion for the Gulf oil spill, investors weren't worried it would bankrupt BP. They barely batted an eye.

"The U.S. government will become insolvent before BP does," said Bruce Lanni, a stock analyst with Nollenberg Capital Partners.

This Internet news story lays out the facts over the first two paragraphs and then delivers a powerful punch line—"They barely batted an eye. . . ."

It also uses strong quotes that move the story ahead. In fact, all three news stories use lively quotes, as well as an active voice and strong verbs (for example, "the White House *arm-twisted* its executives").

> " Play around with technology. Interview other students with a small hand-held camera. It doesn't need to be fancy or expensive. Just playing around with cameras and technology will give journalism students a leg up when they come to college. "
>
> — Carrie Brown, Ph.D., assistant professor of journalism at the University of Memphis

How Do I Become a Reporter?

Here are a few ideas to get you started in the world of journalism:

Get involved. If your high school has a newspaper, become a reporter. If there's no paper, find out how you can start one.

Join the yearbook staff. Volunteer for any and all tasks—photography, caption writing, proofreading, editing, and writing—because these are all skills that modern journalists are required to have. In addition, knowing these skills will make you a better, more well-rounded reporter.

Pitch in. If you have a local newspaper, ask about becoming a student contributor for sports, orchestra, or any area that interests you.

One way to get started as a journalist is to start your own blog, though it's usually a wiser idea to start with learning the tricks of the trade by working on your student newspaper or interning with a professional organization.

Read news stories. Read everything you can—newspapers, magazines, blogs, Twitter feeds. Pay close attention to story ledes and to how stories are structured for different news media.

Start a blog. Be the expert on something you enjoy—skateboarding, cheerleading, marching band, etc. Include personal observations and report on news that others can use when writing about your subject.

Find a summer program. Many universities host summer camps for high school journalism students. To find a program in your state, go to: http://hsj.org/Students/Students.cfm?id=17

Become an intern. Search for intern positions at local magazines and newspapers. Pitch stories to editors again and again and again. Eventually, they will say "yes."

4

Finding Your Niche

YOU MAY HEAR THE WORD "JOURNALIST" and immediately picture a reporter, notebook and pen in hand, covering a big news story such as a war, murder, natural disaster, or stock market crash. And you'd be partially correct—many journalists do bring serious and breaking news to the public.

But journalism includes much more than serious or "hard" news. Journalists also cover arts and entertainment, health, sports, fashion, science, religion, transportation, and countless other topics.

As a budding journalist, you'll have the opportunity to explore many types of journalism. Here is a brief overview of three examples.

Fashion: Successful fashion journalists excel at journalism *and* fashion. By learning how to ask great questions, they can win over sources (experts) and uncover fashion news and trends before the competition.

Bloggers have been added to the agenda at *Teen Vogue*'s annual "Fashion University" meeting.

To get the best stories, fashion journalists cultivate relationships within the fashion industry, including photographers, designers, and public relations specialists. They work closely with editors and photographers to find story ideas and arrange fashion shoots. They pore over press releases, attend fashion shows, visit boutique owners and manufacturers, stay on the lookout for trends, conduct extensive research, and interview people in all areas of the fashion industry.

Health: Health information is much in demand. Pick up any newspaper or magazine or turn on your computer or TV, and you'll find coverage of cancer, Alzheimer's disease, diabetes, obesity, or some other pressing health concern. Health journalism requires reporters who are able to decipher "doctor-speak" and complex medical studies, and explain them in language that the general public can understand. In fact, some of the best health reporters combine a deep interest in science or medicine with a passion for journalism.

Health reporters also cover health and wellness for consumer websites, magazines, newspapers, and for TV and radio. There are also opportunities to report health news for job-specific publications known as trade publications, serving doctors, nurses, physician's assistants, dietitians, and many other health-related occupations.

Health reporting is a thriving segment of journalism, whether it's covered in newspapers, magazines, on television, or on the Internet.

While the circulations of many major newspapers have been dropping, many business newspapers have experienced an increase in circulation.

Business: There's always going to be demand for journalists who can interpret the economy and make it relevant to the average consumer. Business journalism tracks, interprets, and analyzes economic developments in the world and how those developments relate to the individual and society.

Business journalism includes personal finance, the workplace, corporate stability, unemployment, and other economic indicators. Business journalism holds corporations accountable to investors and exposes fraud and risky investments. Business journalists watch international and national trends in the economy and explain how they relate to the consumer's personal financial health.

Business journalists write for a variety of consumer publications as well as business-to-business publications that cover specific industries—from landscaping and construction to computers and technology.

News versus Opinion

News stories may be presented as fact or opinion, depending on where the story appears and on its intent. For example, the election of a U.S. president will spark a variety of news stories about the incoming president—how many people voted, whether states voted for Candidate A or Candidate B, and what the new president hopes to accomplish during his first three months in office.

The same election also will prompt opinion stories in the form of editorials and columns. For example, the election of Candidate A will encourage articles to be written by those for and against that candidate.

Code of Conduct

Whether you're reporting about the war in Afghanistan or the heart-healthy benefits of seafood, your work should be guided by a strong code of ethics.

In fact, every day, reporters, editors, publishers, and news agencies confront some pretty tough ethical questions. Like medicine, law, and many other professions, journalism has ethical codes that focus on the moral aspects of behavior. In fact, many publications and professional associations have codes of ethics for members. The best known in journalism may be that of the Society of Professional Journalists (SPJ). This voluntary code asks members to serve the public with thoroughness and honesty while seeking the truth and providing a fair and comprehensive account of events and issues.

The SPJ code of ethics asks journalists to:

Seek truth and report it by checking for accuracy, distinguishing between advocacy and news reporting, giving subjects of stories the right to respond to allegations of wrongdoing, identifying sources whenever possible, questioning motives of sources and much more;

Minimize harm by treating sources, subjects, and colleagues with respect, compassion, and sensitivity;

Act independently by staying free of obligation to any interest other than the public's right to know;

Be accountable to readers, listeners, viewers, and each other.

Ultimately, ethics is a personal choice about right and wrong. Many actions that are legal are not ethical. For example, while it is legal to name a victim of rape if the name was obtained from court records, an ethical journalist would still withhold the name of an innocent person who has been wronged, because naming them could hurt the victim even more.

5 *Putting It All Together*

NOW THAT YOU'VE LEARNED ABOUT journalism and what goes into a news story, it's time to write your own. Maybe you have some great ideas that you can't wait to report. Or maybe you need a little inspiration. Here are some ideas to get you started:

1. Graduation day is just around the corner. What will students do next? Write a five-hundred-word story about graduating seniors and their plans for the future. Poll the students: How many will go to college? Where will they go? How many will look for full-time jobs? What kinds of jobs will they pursue? What about travel? Will some students take some time to visit other countries or tour the United States?

2. You've seen many different fashion styles in your school, from preppy to punk to vintage. Write a story

about the fashion styles, including where students shop, what students think clothes say about their personalities, and how styles have changed over the last decade. Get out your video camera and interview those students and teachers who have the most intriguing fashion ideas.

3. Studies show that driving while texting can be deadly—for the driver as well as other motorists. Write a story about this dangerous practice, and make sure to include interviews with students who text while driving, national statistics about texting-related traffic incidents, and, if possible, interview somebody who was injured—or had a close call—because of texting behind the wheel.

4. Student Council elections happen once a year. Here's your chance to interview the candidates for class president. Interview them on camera or write a news story, asking about their goals for the upcoming year and why they believe they would make the best class president.

5. Many students volunteer for their favorite charities, such as the local food bank, animal shelter, or nursing home. Write a story about these volunteers. Find out why they chose a particular cause and what motivates them to help others.

6. Write an opinion piece about an issue that you're passionate about, such as cyberbullying. Research the topic and include statistics to support your position, as

well as anecdotes from students who've been victimized. Don't overuse the word "I" in your opinion piece; the facts you present—and how you present them—should clue the reader in to your opinion.

7. Write a movie review. Bring a notebook to the theater and take notes on everything, including the story line, quality of acting, music, audience reaction, and cinematography. When you sit down to write your review, keep in mind that you're going to critique the movie and give your opinion—you're *not* going to give readers a scene-by-scene retelling of events, or give away surprises. For inspiration, go online and read reviews of other movies.

Don't Forget!

Always check and double-check the spelling of names and places. Make sure that numbers, including telephone and address, are accurate.

Make sure all dates are accurate.

Proofread your copy carefully. Don't rely on your computer's spell-checker to find all mistakes.

Fix any grammar or spelling mistakes before you submit your story.

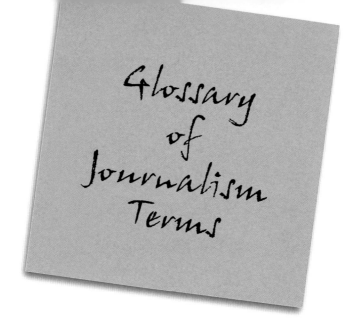

AP Style: The rules included in the *Associated Press Stylebook*, a must-have reporter's handbook on spelling, grammar, punctuation, and usage.

balance: Presenting different viewpoints in a news story so that all sides receive fair coverage.

beat: Area assigned to a reporter for ongoing coverage, such as a sports, politics, legal, health, travel, or entertainment.

byline: Name of the reporter who wrote the story, often placed at the beginning of the published article.

citizen journalism: The publication of news and information by individuals without formal journalism training or professional affiliation. For example, posting cell phone photos or videos from a breaking news event would be considered "citizen journalism," as would blog reports by a citizen covering local sports or city council meetings.

correspondent: Reporter who sends news from outside the newspaper office. A foreign correspondent, for example, sends news from other countries.

cutline: Explanatory words under a photograph or illustration, commonly known as a caption.

deadline: The date and time by which a news report or article must be submitted.

direct quote versus **indirect quote:** Direct quotes provide the exact words used by the person who is being quoted. Quotation marks are required for a direct quote. For indirect quotes, the reporter summarizes what someone else has said, thus no quotation marks are required. In both cases, the information is attributed to the source.

feature: Story emphasizing the human or entertaining aspects of a news story. Features attempt to involve the reader on an emotional level and often have a more flexible time element than a "hard news" story.

freelance journalist: A non-staff reporter, writer, or editor who sells services to publishers without a long-term commitment or full-time job benefits.

hard news: News typically about politics, crime, court cases, or disasters that are of-the-moment and have a strict deadline. Hard news is commonly called "breaking news."

lead: A kernel of information that could turn into a larger story. For example: "I just got a lead on a possible story about contaminants in the water supply. An anonymous caller tells me to check out the Water Department's public records for the past eighteen months." Also common spelling for the first section in a news story.

lede: First section of a news story.

off-the-record: Material offered to the reporter in strict confidence and not for publication; can sometimes be used as general background in a story, if the information is verified by more than one off-the-record source, or cited as coming from a source who spoke on the condition of anonymity.

sidebar: Brief story, often boxed or shaded, that elaborates on a nearby story, providing additional or related news.

source: A person or organization that provides information to the reporter.

stringer: A part-time or freelance correspondent for a publication.

Here's an abbreviated timeline of some important dates in American journalism history:

1608: Captain John Smith becomes the first English reporter in the colonies with the publication of his newsletter, *Newes from Virginia*.

1690: After one issue, *Publick Occurrences, Both Forreign and Domestick*, the first American newspaper, is shut down by the British monarchy and all copies are destroyed.

1704: In the American colonial city of Boston, a newspaper prints advertising.

1729: Ben Franklin makes headlines for more than electricity: His *Pennsylvania Gazette* boasts the largest circulation, most pages, and greatest ad dollars.

1776: The Declaration of Independence appears in more than twenty newspapers.

1783: The *Pennsylvania Evening Post* debuts as the first daily newspaper.

Journalism

1791: The First Amendment to the Constitution is approved, protecting freedom of the press and other speech.

1827: Reporters from three newspapers become the first Washington correspondents.

1849: Newspapers join together in support of a news-gathering service (later known as the Associated Press) that will provide foreign news.

1851: *The New York Times* is founded by Henry Jarvis Raymond and George Jones, who declare, "We publish today the first issue of the New-York Daily Times, and we intend to issue it every morning (Sundays excepted) for an indefinite number of years to come."

1856: *New Orleans Daily Creole* debuts as the first African-American daily newspaper.

1860s: Civil War reporters develop the "summary lead" to ensure that the main point of the news story gets through by telegraph; photographers are issued press passes to cover the war.

1861: Major dailies, including *The New York Times*, publish Sunday issues due to consumer demand for Civil War news. The *Times*, as a leading member of the Associated Press, arranges for the agency to be the official receiver of all war news from the government. Prior to that, the government dished out news to a chosen few news agencies.

1870–1900: Telephones and typewriters change the way work is done in the newsroom; as a result, the number of daily newspapers quadruples.

Cables linking the United States to England and parts of Asia speed news-gathering. Photographs appear in newspapers.

1910–1914: Number of U.S. newspapers reaches new high, with 2,600 dailies and approximately 14,000 weeklies.

1930s: Gossip columns appear for the first time in newspapers; picture magazines such as *LIFE* become popular and open up opportunities for photojournalists.

1930s–1940s: Movie houses show newsreels.

1950s: Television becomes a major source of news. During the late 1940s and early 1950s, television viewers watched news on one of four networks: NBC, CBS, ABC, and DuMont.

1960s: Alternative, or "underground," newspapers start to surge, taking aim at established newspapers as well as the country's political and social structures.

1960–1990: Investigative reporters dig deep for information about government, businesses, events and issues, including organized crime, Watergate and Iran-Contra.

1970s: Computers begin to change the way newspapers are produced—an important early step in the evolution of new media and online journalism.

1980s: The number of daily newspapers decreases due to rising cost of newsprint, rising pay, and a decline in ad revenues.

1989: An online service, which was launched a year earlier by the Quantum company, is renamed America Online. By 1994, the America Online dial-up service has one million subscribers.

Journalism

1990s: Newspaper groups such as Gannett, Knight-Ridder, Condé Nast, New York Times, and Dow Jones own most of the daily papers in the United States. Publishers look for new ways to make money from electronically stored newspaper libraries. By 1990, about 165 U.S. and Canadian daily newspaper companies have news libraries stored electronically. Publishers begin to consider ways to make money from these databases. Reporters now file stories from around the world using laptops and modems or via satellite.

2000 to Present: More and more people are getting their news online for free. With headlines such as "Who Killed the Newspaper?" and "Do Newspapers Have a Future?" newspapers struggle to retain paid readership and advertising. Publishers scramble to create engaging interactive online sites.

2009: First photo of the crash landing of a U.S. Airways plane into the Hudson River is captured with an iPhone and sent via Twitter. Newspapers and magazines widely available on electronic devices, such as the Kindle.

2010: Six in ten Americans get some news online in a typical day; most of these also get news from other media sources such as newspapers, TV, and radio. Facebook becomes the fourth largest source of traffic to news sites, after Google, Yahoo, and MSN. YouTube interviews President Barack Obama, marking the first time that a sitting president is interviewed by social media. Journalism is transforming into something more interactive, where the consumer is also a producer.

Introduction

p. 5, "As a news medium . . . ": Kristen Purcell, Lee Rainie, Amy Mitchell, Tom Rosenstiel, Kenny Olmstead, "Understanding the Participatory News Consumer," Pew Internet & American Life Project, March 1, 2010. www.pewInternet.org/Reports/2010/Online-News.aspx?r=1

Chapter 1

p. 9, "Historians generally credit . . . ": Jeremy Norman, "Acta Diurna: the First Daily Gazette (Circa 131 BCE)." www.histo ryofscience.com/G2I/timeline/index.php?id=1636

p. 10, "The invention of the printing . . . ": Johannes Weber, "Strasburg 1605: The Origins of the Newspaper in Europe," *German History* Vol. 24, Issue 3 (2006): 387–412. http://gh.oxfordjournals.org/cgi/content/abstract/24/3/387

p. 10, "America's first newspaper . . . ": W. David Sloan and Lisa Mullikin Parcell, eds. *American Journalism: History, Principles, Practices,* Jefferson, NC: McFarland & Company, Inc. 2002.

pp. 10–11, "there are approximately . . . ": Newspaper Association of America, "Total Paid Circulation." www.naa.org/Trendsand Numbers/Total-Paid-Circulation.aspx

p. 11, "While newspapers . . . ": Audit Bureau of Circulations, US Newspaper Circulation 2009 data, March 31, 2010. http://abcas3.accessabc.com/ecirc/newstitlesearchus.asp

p. 12, "Historians mark . . . ": "The Trial of Peter Zenger," U.S. History Pre-Columbian to the New Millenium, Philadelphia: Independence Hall Association, 2010. www.ushistory.org/us/7c.asp

p. 14, "Congress shall make no . . . ": The National Archives, *The Bill of Rights*, 1789. www.archives.gov/exhibits/charters/bill_of_rights_transcript.html

p. 22, "Technology is changing . . . ": Vinton G. Cerf, "How the Internet is Changing the Concept of Journalism," *Innovation Journalism*, Issue 3, No. 4 (May 29 2006). www.innovationjournalism.org/archive/INJO-3-4/cerf.pdf

p. 23, "Many news executives . . . ": Pew Research Project's Center for Excellence in Journalism, "News Executives, Skeptical of Government Subsidies, See Opportunity in Technology but Are Unsure About Revenue and the Future, April 12, 2010." www.journalism.org/analysis_report/news_leaders_and_future

Chapter 2

p. 33, "I decided on . . . ": Diane Suchetka, e-mail message to author, March 10, 2010.

pp. 43–44, "I remember meeting . . . ": Angie Lau, e-mail message to author, June 3, 2010.

Chapter 3

p. 53, "Clear, well-organized writing is . . . ": Carrie Brown, e-mail message to author, May 26, 2010.

pp. 56–57, "I wish I'd . . . ": Sara Altshul, e-mail message to author, April 27, 2010.

p. 58, "A healthy seventeen-year-old . . . ": Jonathan Bor, "It Fluttered and Became Bruce Murray's Hearth," *Syracuse Post-Standard,* May 12, 1984. http://blog.syracuse.com/healthfitness/2009/05/fluttered.pdf

p. 58, "I have to . . . ": Chip Scanlan, "The Power of Leads," *Poynter Online,* May 20, 2003. www.poynter.org/column.asp?id=52&aid=35609

p. 61, "I decided to . . . ": Jennifer Hopfinger, e-mail message to author, March 2, 2010.

p. 62, "April 20, 2010 — Oil . . . ": *New York Times* article.

pp. 62–63, "It was in . . . ": *Newsweek* article.

pp. 63–64, "NEW YORK — BP holds . . . ": *Yahoo! News* article.

p. 64, "Play around with . . . ": Carrie Brown, e-mail message to author, May 26, 2010.

The following sources were used to create the Journalism Timeline found on pages 81–84:

University of Minnesota Media History Project, May 18, 2007. www.mediahistory.umn.edu/timeline/1700-1799.html

E. Emery, M. Emery, with N. L. Roberts, *The Press and America: An Interpretive History of the Mass Media,* 8th ed. Boston: Allyn and Bacon, 1996.

David Shedden, "New Media Time Line (1969–2010)," Poynter Online, September 1, 2010. www.poynter.org/content/content_view.asp?id=75953&sid=26

Jeremy Norman, "News Media/Journalism Timeline." www.history ofscience.com/G2I/timeline/index.php?category=News+Media+%2 F+Journalism

All websites were accessible and accurate as of November 12, 2010.

Further
Information

Books

Briggs, Mark. *Journalism Next: A Practical Guide to Digital Reporting and Publishing.* Washington, DC: CQ Press, 2009.

Grundy, Bruce. *So You Want to be a Journalist?*, Cambridge, UK: Cambridge University Press, 2007.

Luckie, Mark S. *The Digital Journalist's Handbook.* Seattle, WA: CreateSpace, 2010.

DVD

The Edward R. Murrow Collection: The McCarthy Years, hosted by Walter Cronkite, New Video Group, 2005.

Websites

High School Journalism Initiative

www.hsj.org

Presented by the American Society of Newspaper Editors, hsj.org is a scholastic journalism site for students, teachers and advisers, guidance counselors, and professional journalists.

High School Journalism News Website

www.myhsj.org

The world's largest host of teen-generated news, this site is connected to more than three thousand student news outlets. It hosts stories, photos, podcasts, and video and other multimedia journalism.

Books

Kovach, Bill, and Tom Rosenstiel. *The Elements of Journalism: What Newspeople Should Know and the Public Should Expect.* New York: Three Rivers Press, 2007.

Paterno, Susan F. and Stein, M. L. *The Newswriter's Handbook.* Ames: Iowa State University Press, 1998.

Reque, John, et al., *Introduction to Journalism.* Evanston, IL: McDougal Littell, 2001.

Sloan, W. David, and Lisa Mullikin Parcell. *American Journalism: History, Principles, Practices.* Jefferson, NC: McFarland & Company, Inc., Publishers, 2002.

Websites

The Journalism Education Association
www.jea.org
Newspaper Association of America Foundation
www.naafoundation.org
Reporters Without Borders: For Press Freedom
http://en.rsf.org/
Society of Professional Journalists
www.spj.org

All websites were accessible and accurate as of November 12, 2010.

Index

Page numbers in boldface are photographs.
Proper names of fictional characters are shown by (C).

16 mm film, 18

accountability, 74
accuracy, 9, 35, 41, 54, 73
Acta Diurna, 9
action words, using, 55, 59, 64
Albarghouti, Jamal, 20, 21, **21**
All the President's Men, 27
American Newspaper Publishers Association, 18
Around the World in Eighty Days, 16
article length, 53–54
Associated Press, 18
audience, target, 33–34, 52
audio, 6, 38, 55

backstory, 31
balance, 43–44, 73
Baltimore Sun, 15
beat, 30, 50
Bernstein, Carl, 27
Bill of Rights, 14
blogs, 6, 23, 29, 53, 61, 66, **66**, 69
Bly, Nellie, 16, 24, **25**
   See also Cochrane, Elizabeth
Bourke-White, Margaret, 26
BP oil spill coverage, 62–64
Bradford, William, **13**
breaking news, 29, 68
broadcast journalism, 18–19
business-to-business publications, **71**

Caesar, Julius, 9
caption (cutline), 65
cell phone, 6, 20–21, **21**
Chicago Tribune, 15
Cho, Seung–Hui, 20

citizen journalism, 20–21
Civil War, 15
clichés, 55
clips of writing, 47
CNN, iReport website, 20
Cochrane, Elizabeth, 16, 24,
  25, *See also* Bly, Nellie
code of conduct, 73–74
color, 39
columnist, 25–26, 56, 72
consumer publications, 71
copy, 54, 55
correspondent, 25
Cosby, William, 12
Count Dracula, **10**
  See also Drakul, Vlad Tsepes
critical thinking, 6, 49

deadlines, 8, 52–53, 52
democracy, news media and, 7
Digg, 6, 23
Drakul, Vlad Tsepes, 10, 10
  See also Count Dracula

editing skill, 65
editorials, 72
e-mail, 6, 23
ethics, code of, 6, 73–74

Facebook, 6, 23
fact-finding, 34, 42, **42,** 45
fashion journalists, 68–70,
  70, 75–76

"Fashion University," **69**
feature story, 33, 53
filing a story, 50
The Final Days, 27
five Ws, and H, of journalism,
  45, 46, 48, 57, 59
Franklin, Benjamin, 12
Franklin, James, 11, 12
freelance journalist, 47, 57,
  61
free press, origin, 12–14, 13

Gandhi, Mohandas K., 26
Gellhorn, Martha, 25
Google News, 61
graphics, as Internet tool, 55
Great Depression, 16, 26

Hamilton, Andrew, 12, 13
hard news, 68
harm, minimizing, 73, 74
Hauptmann, Bruno, **17**
headlines, 30, 31
Hearst, William Randolph,
  15, 16
Hemingway, Ernest, 25
high-speed printing press, 14
home pages, 6

IMDB, 61
InDesign, 6
Industrial Revolution, 14
information provision, 7

Journalism

Internet, 5, 11, 29, 70, **70**
  citizen journalism on, 23
  elements of a news story
    for, 49, 53–55, **54**
  inaccuracy of, 35, 54
  news coverage style, 62–64
  public conversation, 6, 23
  research on, 34, 35
  social media tools, 6, 23
  unlimited time/space
    advantage, 22, **22**
internship, 66, 67
interview, 6, 8, 29, 41, 76
  how-to techniques, 36–39
  local community, 30, **30**
  for reliable research, 36
  video, 32, 76
inverted pyramid, 44
investigative reporter, 24, 25

job-specific publications, 70
journalism
  American style, 10–12
  balance, 43–44
  basic elements of, 6, 29–30
  five Ws, and H of, 45, 46, 48
  getting quotes, 39–40
  interviewing, 36–39
  reasons for entering, 5,
    7–8, 28, 33, 61
  researching a story, 34–36
  story ideas, 30–32
  target audience, 33–34

  technology and, 6
journalism education, 6
journalism, niche types of,
  business, 71, **71**
  fashion, 68–69, **69**
  health, 70, **70**
journalists
  brave, 24–27, 25
  characteristics of, 28–29

Kennedy, John F., 19

laptop, 6, 29
layout design software, 6
lead (lede), 8, 29, 31, 44–45,
  55, 57–58, 62, 66
libel, 12–13
library, research and, 34
LIFE magazine, 26
Lindbergh, Charles, 17
Lindbergh baby kidnapping,
  16, 17, **17**
links, 6, 55
Lovejoy, Elijah, 24

magazines, 47, 61, 66, 70, **70**
  general interest, 50
  internships, 67
  narrow-interest, 50
  news, 11, 29
  news coverage style, 62–63
  story elements for, 49,
    50, 52–53, **52**

mass readership, 14–15, 16
mixed metaphors, 55
mobile uploads, 23

New England Courant, 11, 12
news, characteristics of, 6
news beat, 30, 50
Newseum, **21**
news gathering
  "creating" news, 15–16, 24
  expanded stories, 31
  newspapers, tradition of, 11
news media, story structuring
  for differing, 62–64, 66
newspapers, 5, 9, 29, 61, 66,
  70, **70**
  business, 71
  competition to, 18
  elements of a news story
    for, 49, 50, 51
  first known, 10
  history of American, 10–12
  internship, 67
  large, 30
  long tradition of, 11
  news coverage style, 62
  small, 30, 33, 34, 47, 50
  space limitations, 22
  student, 34–35, 65, 66
  website, 29
news reporting, objective, 11
news sheets, 10
Newsweek, 62–63

newsworthy, deciding, 11
news writing, craft of,
  basic skills of, 6
  crafting a lead, 57–58
  practice and, 53
  supporting paragraphs,
    59–60
  tips for successful, 55
New York Journal, 15
New York Weekly Journal, 12
New York World, 15
New York Times, 15, 62
niche, 52, 61, 68–71
Nixon, Richard M., **19**, 27
Nixon-Kennedy presidential
  debates, 19, **19**
nonessential details, 45, 57
note-taking, 29, 38, **38**, 59

objectivity, 6, 11, 43–44
opinion stories, 76–77
  forms of, 72
  vs. news, 16, 72

penny press, 14–15
Pew Internet & American Life
  Project, 5
Phileas Fogg (C), 16
photography, 29
photojournalists, 26
Photoshop, 6
Plain Dealer, 33
police news, 33

Journalism

press, freedom of, 7–8, 12–14,
  13
press reform, 16
press releases, 69
print journalism
  space limitations, 22
  survival, adaptation and, 23
print sources, research, 34
proofreading, 65
propaganda, 11, 12
*Publick Occurrences, Both
  Foreign and Domestick*, 11
public opinion, influences, 12
Pulitzer, Joseph, 15
Pulitzer Prize, 27
Pyle, Ernie, 25–26

quotes, 29, 39–40, 45, 59–61
  interview techniques, 36
  paraphrasing, 40
  purpose of, 43, 60, 62, 64

radio, 5, 11, 18, 22, 29, 70
reader interaction, via social
  media, 6
reporter
  earliest, 9
  investigative, 24, 25
  specialized, 30, 68–71
  tips on becoming a, 65–67
reporting
  basic skills of, 6
  newspapers, tradition of, 11

researching a story, 29, 34–36
  angles to pursue, 35
  background on subject, 37
  fact-finding, 34
Revolutionary War, 12, 14
run-on sentences, 55

Scripps, E. W., 16
sedition, 13
sensationalism, 11, 15, 16
  See also yellow journalism
serious news, 68
slanting news, 43
social media, interaction, 6
Society of Professional
  Journalists (SPJ), 73
software, 6
source, 37, 39, 45, 68
  confirming facts, 42
  credible, 59
  identifying, 73
  print, for research, 34
  trustworthyness of, 35
Spanish Civil War, 25
spelling, 41
still shots, 6
story ideas, finding, 30–32
story placement, 30, 31, 51
summer programs, 67

tabloid, 16
target audience, 33–34, 52
technology, 14–15, 22–23, 64

Teen Vogue, 69, **69**
teleprompter, 18–19
television, 11, 29, 70, 70
  local/national, 5
  time limitations on, 22
text, 6
trade publications, 70
trends
  business, 71
  from current events, 32
  fashion, 68, 69
Twain, Mark, 15
Twitter, 6, 23, 66

United States Constitution
  Bill of Rights, 14
  First Amendment, 14

Verne, Jules, 16
video, 6, 29
  capturing/editing, 6
  cell phone, 20–21, 21
  as Internet tool, 55
videojournalism, 32
Vietnam War, 19, 25

Virginia Tech massacre, 20–21,
  21
voice, active vs. passive, 55,
  59, 64

Wall Street Journal, 11
war correspondent, 25
Washington Post, 27
"watchdog" media, 7
Watergate, 19, 27
websites, 31, 35–36, 47, 61
  consumer, 70
  iReport, CNN, 20
  newspaper, 29
  for summer programs, 67
Woodward, Bob, 27
word of mouth, accuracy, 9
World War I, 16
World War II, 25, 26

Yahoo! News (Internet),
  63–64
yellow journalism, 15

Zenger, John Peter, 12, 13, **13**

About the Author

JULIE A. EVANS is a journalist who lives in Cleveland Heights, Ohio. She writes articles about family and healthy living for websites, magazines, and books. Her work has appeared in *Better Homes & Gardens*, *Prevention*, *Fitness*, *Best Life*, 360-5.com, and many other publications.